Helping Children See Jesus

ISBN: 978-1-64104-063-1

Eternal Salvation
*New Testament Volume 35:
Hebrews, Part Two*

Authors: R. Iona Lyster and Maureen Pruitt
Illustrator: Frances H. Hertzler
Colorization Courtesy of Good Life Ministries
Page Layout: Patricia Pope

© 2019 Bible Visuals International
PO Box 153, Akron, PA 17501-0153
Phone: (717) 859-1131
www.biblevisuals.org

All rights reserved. No part of this publication may be reproduced, stored in a retrieval system or transmitted in any form by any means, electronic, mechanical, photocopy, recording or otherwise, without the prior permission of the publisher, except as provided by USA copyright law.

RELATED ITEMS

To access related items (such as activities, memory verse posters and translated texts) please visit our web store at www.biblevisuals.org and enter 1035 at the top right of the web page. You may need to reduce the zoom setting to get the search box.

FREE TEXT DOWNLOAD

To obtain a FREE printable copy of the English teaching text (PDF format) under Product Format, please scroll down and select Extra–PDF Teacher Text Download. Then under Language select English before clicking the ADD TO CART button to place in your shopping cart. Other languages are available at an additional cost from the Language menu. When checking out, use coupon code XTACSV17 at checkout and click on Apply Coupon to receive the discount on the English text.

Jesus Christ

the same yesterday, and to day, and forever.

Hebrews 13:8

Lesson 1
OUR NEED OF SALVATION

NOTE TO THE TEACHER

Salvation is an extremely important doctrine which must be clearly understood. A curse is placed on anyone (even an angel!) who does not tell the true gospel. (See Galatians 1:8-9.) So the gospel of salvation must be explained accurately.

Salvation includes: (1) forgiveness of sins of the *past* (Romans 1:16); (2) power to overcome sin in this *present* life (Romans 6:14); and (3) *future* deliverance from the sin nature (Romans 8:29; 1 John 3:2). Salvation is by grace through faith. It is a gift–entirely free from works (Ephesians 2:8-9). Salvation comes first; works follow salvation (Titus 3:5-8).

Salvation depends upon the Saviour, the Lord Jesus Christ. On earth, He proved He is sinless. By His death, He, the perfect One, took the punishment sinners deserve. He was our substitute. (See Matthew 20:28; Mark 10:45; 1 Peter 2:24.)

More than 200 times in the New Testament, it is declared that salvation is received by faith alone. (See, for example, Ephesians 2:8-9.) This faith must be placed in the Lord Jesus Christ. (See John 3:16; Acts 16:31.) Salvation is a free gift. Therefore, we who teach must *never* suggest that we give God anything. *He* gives it all.

We receive this gift by placing our trust in His Son. (See John 1:12.) To teach any different gospel from that of salvation by grace through faith, comes under the curse of Galatians 1:8-9. This is the strongest kind of warning!

This glorious salvation purchased by Christ with His own precious blood, lasts forever. It is eternal salvation. The moment a person is saved, the Holy Spirit places him in the body of Christ eternally (1 Corinthians 12:13). The believer is forever sealed by the Holy Spirit who dwells within the believer. (See Ephesians 1:13; 4:30.) The Father keeps the true believer eternally (John 10:28-30). One day in His own presence believers will be presented faultless (Jude 24). No believer can be accused of anything that would cause him to lose his salvation. God is the Judge of all. And He has already pronounced believers righteous–in right standing with Himself (Romans 8:33-34). Our Lord is continually making intercession for His own. That is enough to keep each true believer saved. God's Word promises that nothing can separate the believer from the love of God which is in Christ Jesus the Lord. (See Romans 8:29-39.) May every student you teach truly receive salvation and have the joy of knowing it is his forever!

Scripture to be studied: Hebrews 2:1-18; Luke 15:1-10

The *aim* of the lesson: To explain what salvation is and how it is obtained.

What your students should *know*: Christ is the only Saviour.

What your students should *feel*: A desire to receive Christ and His gift of salvation.

What your students should *do*:
Unsaved: Place their trust in Christ and receive salvation.
Saved: Thank God for this great salvation which brings deliverance from sin and Satan.

Lesson outline (for the teacher's and students' notebooks):

1. Salvation: what it is (Luke 15:1-10).
2. The need for salvation (Romans 3:10-23; Hebrews 2:5-8).
3. Christ makes salvation possible (Hebrews 2:9-16; Revelation 13:8).
4. The blessings of salvation (Hebrews 2:11-13; 7:26b).

The verse to be memorized:

How shall we escape, if we neglect so great salvation?
(Hebrews 2:3a)

THE LESSON

What do you suppose the Hebrews (Jews) thought when they read the letter addressed to them? (That letter is now part of the Bible and is entitled *The Epistle to the Hebrews*.) It was written by the hand of a man. Do you think the Jews knew it actually came from God? (*Teacher:* Encourage discussion.)

The prophets, angels, and Moses were extremely important to the Hebrews. But God wanted them to know that His Son, the Lord Jesus Christ, is far better than all others. Because He is the greatest messenger of God, His message is greatest. So the Hebrews did much thinking when they heard this read: "We ought to give more careful attention to the things we have heard. If we do not, we may slip away from them." (See Hebrews 2:1.)

What wonderful truths many Jews had heard! Years before in their holy city (Jerusalem) the Lord Jesus told them, "I am the door: by Me if anyone enter in, he shall be saved"... "I am the good shepherd: the good shepherd gives His life for the sheep"... "I lay down my life for the sheep"... "I give unto them eternal life; and they shall never perish, neither shall any man pluck them out of My hand... and no man is able to pluck them out of My Father's hand." (See John 10:9, 11, 15, 28-29.)

Hearing the Lord Jesus, many Jewish people turned to Him and received eternal life. Others, however, drifted away from His truths. So, God's Spirit reminded them (in the Letter): "How can anyone, who neglects the salvation which the Lord has provided, escape His penalty?" (See Hebrews 2:2-3.) This was a sobering thought. For simply *neglecting* salvation, God would punish them!

In most Hebrew homes, these matters were discussed. The children would have been full of questions. "What did the Letter mean, Father, when it spoke of salvation?"

1. SALVATION: WHAT IT IS
Luke 15:1-10

"Salvation has several meanings. For example, it means *to find the lost*. Suppose a child gets lost in the woods. He runs this way and that but cannot find the right way. Exhausted, he drops to the ground and cries himself to sleep. The men of the village search until they find him. The lost is found. And that is part of the meaning of the word salvation: *to find the lost*."

Father continued, "Salvation means also *to rescue*. Suppose you are drowning. You have gone under the water once, twice, three times. I jump in and struggle back to shore with you in my arms. We pump the water out of you. You breathe again. Your life is saved. What would you tell your friends?"

"I would tell them, 'My father saved me.' "

"Of course you would," the father said. "And that word *saved* is included in the meaning of salvation. *Someone is rescued.*"

"Salvation means also *to keep safe*. Suppose you want something very much. (*Teacher:* Name an article your students desire.) You work hard and save your money so you will be able to buy it. What do you do with that hard-earned money in the meantime? You keep it in a safe place. And that, too, is part of the meaning of salvation: *to keep safe*."

Show Illustration #1a

The father continued, "When the Lord Jesus was here on earth, He said one of His reasons for coming from Heaven was 'to seek and to save that which was lost' (Luke 19:10). Earlier he had told the story of a sheep which wandered from its shepherd. It went its own way, getting farther and farther from the shepherd."

"But the shepherd loved that wandering sheep. He climbed up the hills. He plunged through the thicket, down into the valleys. He crossed rivers. Always he was calling, calling, calling. Finally he heard a pitiful, weak 'Baa!' He found his one lost sheep. Putting it on his shoulder, he carried it back to safety. The sheep had been lost. The shepherd *found it*. It had been in danger. The shepherd *saved it*. That is salvation. Is this clear?" the father wanted to know.

"Oh, yes, I understand. The sheep could not help itself. It needed the shepherd to find it and take it home."

"Right you are!" the father said encouragingly. "And that is what the Lord Jesus meant when He said, 'The good Shepherd gives His life for the sheep.' When the Shepherd, Jesus, died on the cross, He gave His life for us, the sheep."

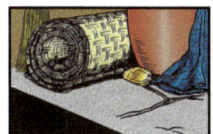
Show Illustration #1b

Father continued, "The Lord Jesus told another story about a certain woman who had ten silver coins. Because she received them from her husband when they were married, the coins were precious to her. She doubtless wore them on a chain on her forehead. One day one of the coins disappeared. Being very upset, she searched every corner of the house with the aid of a candle. Suddenly something reflected the candlelight. It was her coin! She seized it and ran outside calling to her friends, 'Come! Look! I have found the coin which was lost!' What a happy time they had! Do you think she took good care of all her coins after that?"

"Oh, yes! She would have fastened them securely, making certain they were safe."

"Exactly. And that is included in the meaning of salvation. Someone *in safe keeping* is *saved*. When the Lord Jesus spoke of the Good Shepherd, He said, 'I give unto them eternal life; and they will never perish, neither will any man pluck them out of My hand . . . and no man is able to pluck them out of My Father's hand.' He and God the Father hold saved ones *safely forever* (see John 10:28-29). This is the kind of salvation God provides–eternal salvation."

2. THE NEED FOR SALVATION
Romans 3:10-23; Hebrews 2:5-8

The family listened thoughtfully. The father added, "The letter addressed to us Hebrews tells the importance of human beings. In the beginning God gave angels a high place in creation. He made man a little lower in rank. He made him in the image of God. And God put him–Adam–in charge. Everything on earth was to obey Adam. (See Hebrews 2:7-8.) And Adam was to obey God."

Show Illustration #2

Father continued, "But instead of obeying God, Adam and his wife Eve listened to Satan, the enemy of God. Satan wanted to spoil what God had made. He wanted man to sin. When Adam and Eve listened to Satan and chose to disobey God, they sinned. So Adam could no longer rule over God's creation. And he had to be punished for his sin."

"We are exactly like Adam and Eve. We choose to disobey God. And this is sin. Like the sheep and the coin the Lord Jesus told about, we are lost. We need Someone to rescue us and keep us safe and secure forever."

3. CHRIST MAKES SALVATION POSSIBLE
Hebrews 2:9-16; Revelation 13:8

The children edged closer to their father. He spoke softly. "Before the world was made, God the Father and God the Son planned a way to save us. The Son would come to earth as a man and live through everything that we have to live through.

Show Illustration #3

"He would he hungry, lonely, poor, tormented, tortured, laughed at. He, the perfect One, would take the punishment for the sin of all people everywhere. To rescue us, He would pay with His blood by dying on the cross. He would conquer sin and death by rising from the dead."

4. THE BLESSINGS OF SALVATION
Hebrews 2:11-13; 7:25b

"You mean Christ knew He would die, even before the world began?" the youngest child wanted to know.

"Yes, He did. But the Letter to us Hebrews says He 'tasted' death for everyone (Hebrews 2:9). Jesus drank the cup of death in our place."

Show Illustration #4

"But the Lord Jesus did not stay dead. He arose, proving He had conquered death," their father continued.

"Now Christ is sitting at the right hand of God the Father in Heaven, crowned with glory and honor" (Hebrews 2:9; Acts 2:33-34; Romans 8:34; Ephesians 1:20; Colossians 3:1; Hebrews 1:3, 13; 8:1; 10:12; 12:2; 1 Peter 3:22).

"What is He doing there?" the oldest son asked.

"He is talking to God about us. He is praying for us who belong to Him. And, amazingly enough, He speaks of us as His brothers. We belong to His family and He is not ashamed of us. (See Hebrews 2:11-13.) Imagine that! We do many things which make us ashamed of ourselves. But He keeps right on caring for us and talking to God about us. And do you know why?"

"Because He loves us," the children chorused.

And this is true! The Lord Jesus does love us. We shall never understand what it cost Him to rescue us from sin and Satan. We may never know why He chose us who have trusted in Him to be in His family. But of this we can be certain: those who place their trust in Him are His forever. No one is able to take them out of His hand. They are saved and safe forever. They have eternal salvation. Have *you* been born into the family of God? The Lord Jesus has done everything He can for you. He has searched for you by sending this message to you right now. You can be rescued from sin by trusting in Him. The moment you are in His family you will be safe forever. He is waiting to give you eternal salvation. Will you place your trust in Him right now?

Lesson 2
SALVATION THROUGH OUR KINSMAN-REDEEMER

NOTE TO THE TEACHER

The *Epistle to the Hebrews* presents salvation in a series of word pictures. At the center of each is Christ, the One who brings salvation. Our lessons on salvation teach the same basic truths: (1) All are lost and need a Saviour. (2) Christ provided salvation for all.

In our last lesson, a lost sheep and a lost coin needed to be found. In this lesson, we see that all people are slaves to sin and need redemption. Last time we learned that Christ is the One who seeks and saves the lost. He is the Saviour. Today we shall see Him as the near relative of man, the Kinsman who redeems the slave. (In this *Visualized Bible* series, the subject of redemption is more fully covered in Old Testament Volume 7.)

We must be careful to present the right balance between God's holiness and His love. He must punish sin but He provides salvation through His Son. God's holiness and His love are both needed to complete the truth of salvation.

Scripture to be studied: Hebrews 2:9-18; Ruth 1:1—4:22

The *aim* of the lesson: To show that to have salvation, a person must have a Redeemer.

What your students should *know*: The Lord Jesus Christ is the Redeemer.

What your students should *feel*: Gratitude for redemption.

What your students should *do*:

Unsaved: Place their trust in the Redeemer and receive salvation.

Saved: Name and pray for a friend with whom they can share the message of salvation this week.

Lesson outline (for the teacher's and students' notebooks):

1. A Kinsman-Redeemer is needed (Ruth 1:19-22).
2. A Kinsman-Redeemer is found (Ruth 2:1-4:22).
3. Christ came to be our Kinsman-Redeemer (Hebrews 2:9-17; 9:12, 22; 12:2).
4. Our Kinsman-Redeemer brings us to God (Hebrews 9:12-15; 10:1-4, 12-17).

The verse to be memorized:

How shall we escape, if we neglect so great salvation? (Hebrews 2:3a)

THE LESSON

Naomi, her husband and two sons lived happily in Bethlehem. (See the Book of Ruth 1:1-18.) Then a famine came. Everyone was hungry. They needed bread. They needed food. They needed water. In the land of Moab (they were told) there was plenty to eat. But there were problems: Naomi and her family were weak from hunger. Walking all the way to Moab (about 160 kilometers) would not be easy. Naomi and her family worshiped the true and living God of Heaven. The people of Moab worshiped worthless gods made of wood and stone. And the Moabites were enemies. What should Naomi and her family do?

Day after day Naomi shook her head sadly when her sons and husband asked for something–anything–to eat. Night after night all four went to bed hungry. Seeing her sick, pining sons was too much for Naomi. Finally the decision was made. They all would go to the land of plenty.

How they enjoyed the good food in Moab! Once again Naomi looked like the meaning of her name: *pleasant*. She missed her homeland. But to be able to feed her family was a great relief. Then one sad day, Naomi's husband died. In time, her sons married Moabite women. Soon, both sons died. Poor Naomi!

Later, she heard that food and water were available in her own land. So Naomi decided to return. Ruth, wife of one of her sons, insisted on going with Naomi. "Where you go, I shall go . . . Your people will be my people, and your God my God," Ruth said.

1. A KINSMAN-REDEEMER IS NEEDED
Ruth 1:19-22

Show Illustration #5

So it was that the sorrowing, bitter Naomi returned to Bethlehem–and Ruth with her. Without husbands, how could they live? Naomi would have to sell her land to get money. According to the law, it would have to be sold to a close relative, a kinsman. There was another problem. Whoever bought the land would have to marry Ruth, for that was the custom. Would anyone want to marry a foreign girl–a girl from Moab? Or must she be sold as a slave?

When a relative bought the land, it was said he *redeemed* it. This meant he bought the land to keep it in the family. When he married the widow of his relative, he *redeemed* her too, so she would not have to be a slave. The man who would do this was called a *kinsman-redeemer*. He was a relative who bought the land and married the widow. Where would a kinsman-redeemer be found for Ruth, the stranger?

2. A KINSMAN-REDEEMER IS FOUND
Ruth 2:1-4:22

Ruth had much to learn about the Jewish laws. Naomi began, "Ruth, God has given us Hebrews a law which will take care of you and me. The law says that when farmers harvest their fields, the poor are allowed to follow them and pick up the grain they leave. (See Leviticus 19:9-10.)

Immediately Ruth knew what she would do. Early the next morning she went to gather food. God led her to the fields of a wealthy man named Boaz. Ruth came home that evening happily carrying a heavy load of grain.

"Where did you get all this?" Naomi asked.

"In the field of a man named Boaz," Ruth answered.

"Oh, Ruth, that is wonderful! Boaz is one of our kinsmen." Naomi was delighted.

Day after day Ruth returned to the fields belonging to Boaz. He watched her as she worked. He was kind to her. Finally Naomi had a suggestion for Ruth: "According to our custom, you must show Boaz you are willing for him to redeem you."

So Ruth followed the custom. She let him know and was disappointed by his reply: "It is true that I am a near kinsman. But there is another kinsman more closely related. I shall have to see if he is able to do what a kinsman ought."

Show Illustration #6

The next morning Boaz went to the city gate and sat down to wait for the other kinsman to come that way. When the man came, Boaz called, "Sit down here!" And the man sat down. Boaz asked others to join them so they could witness what was said. This they did.

Boaz began, "Naomi has a piece of land to sell. Will you redeem it?"

"I'll redeem it," the man answered.

Boaz explained, "When you buy the field from Naomi, you must buy it also from Ruth the Moabitess."

Immediately the man knew he would have to marry Ruth. He answered, "Since that is so, I cannot redeem it for myself. Buy it for yourself."

Could Boaz be Ruth's kinsman-redeemer? Yes, for he was the next nearest relative. Did he have the money to redeem the land and her? Yes, he had the right price. Did he want to redeem her? Oh yes, he certainly did!

So Boaz redeemed the land and married Ruth. From then on, instead of her being a stranger, a foreigner, she was the wife of a wealthy, respected man. She shared all he had: his land, home, love and–best of all–his God. In time a son was born to them. Their son became the grandfather of King David, the great king God gave to the Hebrew nation. Through David, Ruth became one of the ancestors of our Lord Jesus Christ. Ruth had no right to all these blessings. But because Boaz had redeemed her, she received them all.

3. CHRIST CAME TO BE OUR KINSMAN-REDEEMER
Hebrews 2:9-17; 9:12, 22; 12:2

In our last lesson we learned why everyone needs salvation. All people everywhere are lost, like the sheep. Like the coin, all are in darkness. No one is able to save himself. The shepherd had to search for the sheep and rescue it. The woman had to find the coin and put it away safely.

Ruth, a pagan girl, worshiped false, make-believe gods. This made her a slave of sin and Satan. She was in darkness, away from the true God. She was a foreigner, not one of the children of God. But Ruth was saved from all this when Boaz redeemed her.

As Boaz was Ruth's kinsman-redeemer, so the Lord Jesus is our Kinsman-Redeemer. He is all that a kinsman-redeemer must be.

1. *A kinsman-redeemer must be a near relative.* For a time, the Lord Jesus put aside all the glory He had with God in Heaven. (See Hebrews 2:9, 14, 16.) A body was made for Him so He could live on earth as a man. There never was anyone like Jesus Christ–both God and man at the same time. All other men want their own way. They have disobeyed God and sinned. The man, Christ Jesus, obeyed God perfectly. He could honestly say, "I do always those things that please God" (John 8:29).

Show Illustration #7

The night before the Lord Jesus was crucified, He prayed to His Father saying, "Not My will, but Thine be done." And it was the will of God that He who came to earth in a body like ours should take the punishment for our sins. Because He was like us (except for sin), He speaks of us as His "brothers" (Hebrews 2:11-12). He is our kinsman.

2. *A kinsman-redeemer must be able to pay the price to redeem.* Boaz had to pay to redeem Ruth and the land. Christ Jesus, our Kinsman-Redeemer, bought us for a very great price: His own precious blood. (See 1 Peter 1:18-19; also Hebrews 9:12, 22.) Believers are set free forever from the slavery of sin and Satan because of the price Christ paid.

3. *A kinsman-redeemer must be willing to redeem.* One kinsman was not willing to redeem Ruth. But Boaz was willing to do so. Just so, the Lord Jesus was willing to die for sinners. He gladly did so! We are told: " . . . Jesus…who for the joy that was set before Him, endured the cross, despising the shame" (Hebrews 12:2).

4. OUR KINSMAN-REDEEMER BRINGS US TO GOD
Hebrews 9:12-15; 10:1-4, 12-17

In the beginning God created Adam and Eve because He wanted to enjoy them. They talked together as good friends. But the moment Adam and Eve disobeyed God, everything was spoiled. Their sin separated them from Him. Because God is perfectly holy, their sin made them fear Him.

Show Illustration #8

Years later, God spoke again to His people. (See Exodus 19:9-20:26.) But He would not let them get near the mountain from which He spoke. There were thunder, lightning, darkness, fire and smoke. The mountain shook. A trumpet sounded loud and long. If either man or animal even touched the mountain, he died instantly. The people were terrified. Even their courageous leader, Moses, was "exceedingly" afraid. (See Hebrews 12:18-21.) God wanted His people to remember that because He is holy and they were sinful, they were separated from Him.

For hundreds of years sinners offered sacrifices for sins. Thousands, even millions of animals died on altars. Each was a substitute for the one who sinned. But no matter how many animals a sinner offered, his conscience still bothered Him. (See Hebrews 10:1-4.) He was still separated from God.

All this was changed when the Lord Jesus died. In this wonderful letter to the Hebrews we are told that Jesus gave Himself once for sins. That one sacrifice is good forever. He will not remember the redeemed believer's sins and wrong-doings anymore. (See Hebrews 10:12-17.)

Have you ever turned to the Lord Jesus, as Ruth did to Boaz, to say you are willing to be redeemed? He will not force you to accept His salvation. You must turn to Him willingly, just as you are. Like all people everywhere, you are a slave of sin and Satan. You cannot free yourself. You need to be redeemed–set free–by the perfect One who has paid for you with His own precious blood. Will you receive the Redeemer, Jesus Christ the Lord? If you will, He will save you. He will give you everlasting life. You will be His forever.

If you have already trusted in Christ, have you shared the good news of salvation with others? Think now of someone who should be introduced to the Saviour. If you want to mention the name of that person, we'll all pray together that you'll have the opportunity of sharing the gospel with your friend *this* week.

Lesson 3
THE CAPTAIN OF OUR SALVATION

NOTE TO THE TEACHER

Some of the Jewish believers who received *The Epistle to the Hebrews* had a problem. They were wavering in their Christian faith. Many were doubtless second-generation Christians. (See Hebrews 2:3; 13:7.) But they had not grown spiritually as they should have for the length of time they had been trusting in Christ. (See Hebrews 5:12.) Instead of progressing vigorously, they were drifting. The one who wrote the letter knew a great deal about sailing. He warned them that if they were not careful, they would drift ("slip" away) from their Christian teaching. (See Hebrews 2:1.) He encouraged them to "hold fast"–be securely anchored (3:6). Their faith in Christ, he said, was a sure, steadfast anchor (Hebrews 6:19). He told them to beware of shortening their sail. They were to advance in their Christian experience not draw back (10:38). He warned them also against being swept about with the current (13:9).

With equal firmness, the writer explained the reasons for and how to correct drifting:

1. They had lost their first glowing love for Christ and were living lazy Christian lives. (See 5:11-12; 6:12.) To correct this, they would have to judge the value of their salvation. They must remember how much it cost the Lord Jesus to redeem them (12:1-3).

2. Like Christians everywhere in those days, many Jewish believers were persecuted. (See 10:32; 12:3-4; 13:3.) The Roman emperor, Nero, had killed thousands 0f Christians. The increasing danger to the Hebrews was hindering their spiritual growth. To correct this, they constantly would have to remember the sufferings of the Lord. (See 12:2; 13:12.)

3. Some of the Jewish Christians were toying with strange doctrines. (See 13:9.) To correct this, they must remember that the Lord Jesus is forever the same, as is all truth about Him.

Alas, the Hebrews were simply drifting. In this letter they are instructed to move out into the world and call others to follow Christ (13:13-16). They must give vigorous attention to their spiritual growth.

What was written for them is equally true for us.

Scripture to be studied: Hebrews 2:1, 10; 3:6; 5:8-9; 6:19-20; 10:38; 13:9

The *aim* of the lesson: To teach the responsibilities and blessings of having Christ as the Captain of our lives.

What your students should *know*: We need the Captain to control our lives.

What your students should *feel*: A desire to keep their lives pure.

What your students should *do*: Check their lives against Hebrews 13:13-18 and list where they are falling short of God's commands. Mention how they plan to correct these matters in the week ahead.

Lesson outline (for the teacher's and students' notebooks):

1. Drifting believers need to remember their Saviour (Hebrews 5:11-12; 6:12; 12:1-3).
2. Persecuted believers must remember their Lord's sufferings (Hebrews 10:32; 12:2-4; 13:3, 12).
3. Believers may be caught in the current but are fastened to the Rock (Hebrews 13:5-9).
4. Believers are kept safe forever by the Captain of salvation (Hebrews 2:9-10; 7:24-25).

The verse to be memorized:

How shall we escape, if we neglect so great salvation? (Hebrews 2:3a)

THE LESSON

Have you ever drifted in a boat with the sails rolled up? The water is calm. Fluffy clouds float overhead. Gentle breezes carry you along lazily. Down, down the stream you float, slowly, noiselessly. You are drifting and you do not have to do anything.

Long ago the Hebrew Christians were drifting. They were not in a boat, you understand. They were members of the family of God. But they no longer told others about the Lord Christ. Some, apparently, were not even attending God's house regularly. (See Hebrews 10:25.) They were Christian believers who had become careless. They were drifting.

Hundreds of years before the Lord Jesus came to earth, God had chosen the Jewish people in a special way for Himself. He loved them. He cared for them. He provided a special kind of worship for them. Later the Jewish people had a magnificent temple with beautiful furnishings. And a gorgeous veil–oh, how they admired it!

But the moment the Lord Jesus died, God tote the veil from the top to the bottom. Their temple worship could never again be the same. Still they proudly refused to believe that the Lord Jesus Christ is the Son of God. And, in time, one of their leading men did everything he could to get rid of all Christians. (See Acts 8:3; 9:1-2.)

Some Jews did turn to the Lord Jesus–one or two here, a few there. It was not easy for them to wrench away from their families and friends. Christians had no beautiful place to worship. They met simply in one another's homes. (See Acts 20:20.) Instead of observing many feast days, they ate pieces of broken bread and sipped the juice of grapes. No, it was not easy to leave the glorious Jewish ceremonies for the simple Christian meetings. But thousands of Hebrews heard the gospel preached by the apostles. They saw the mighty miracles of the Holy Spirit (Hebrews 2:4). And some truly believed in the Lord Jesus

Christ. Having made their decisions, these believers plowed ahead like boats forging against the rough currents. There was no turning back. For these Jewish Christians loved the Lord Jesus and followed Him gladly.

1. DRIFTING BELIEVERS NEED TO REMEMBER THEIR SAVIOUR
Hebrews 5:11-12; 6:12; 12:1-3

The years passed. Their sons and daughters grew and they, too, turned to the Lord Jesus. Often these children heard their parents speak of the old days when they worshiped God in the beautiful temple. Finally some had an idea: Why not put together the best of the Jewish religion with the Christian faith? They could follow the law given by the great Jewish leader, Moses. They could enjoy the worship of God in the magnificent temple. They would have priests who would go to God for them. They could also have angels praying for them. Thus they could drift along with the Jews *and* the Christians. They were pleased with their ideas. But God was not.

Show Illustration #9

So God caused a man to write them a letter (*The Epistle to the Hebrews*). In it God said that angels, the law, Moses, the temple and priests were important in days gone by. Now, since His Son had come to earth, everything was different. He, the Lord Jesus Christ, is better, greater, more important than all the old Jewish practices. Ever thing Christ said was much greater than the sayings of the prophets. "Stop drifting away from the truths you know," the letter told them. "Think of what it cost the Lord Jesus to leave His glorious Heavenly home to come to earth. Remember the price He paid on the cross to redeem *you*. He has bought *you* with His precious blood. Now, because *you* have trusted in Him, *you* are set free from sin and Satan. And you have the same kind of life He has–eternal, everlasting life. Moses could not do what the Saviour did for you. Nor could the angels or prophets or priests. Forget them! Think what the Lord Jesus did for you. Remember Him alone!" (See Hebrews 2:9-17; 3:1-6; 5:5-10.)

What do you suppose those Jewish Christians thought, and said, and did when they received this message from God? (*Teacher:* Encourage class discussion.)

2. PERSECUTED BELIEVERS MUST REMEMBER THEIR LORD'S SUFFERINGS
Hebrews 10:32; 12:2-4; 13:3, 12

Surely many of the Hebrews did as they were told. But there were some who had another problem. Every day they heard of Christians who, because they trusted in Christ, were being treated cruelly. Some were in jail. Others were severely beaten. Many had been put to death. The Jewish young people loved the Lord Jesus. But to be punished for their faith? There must have been many discussions among them. "How can we be Christians without letting people know we are Christians?" "If we knew our tormenters would put us in jail, would it be all right to lie, saying we are not Christians?" "If a man planned to kill me for worshiping the Lord Jesus, would it be all right for me to kill him first?" "What could we do for Christ if we were in jail? Or only half alive from beatings? Or suppose we were dead. What good would we be to Him? We certainly should not let anyone else know we are Christians." So the talk went on and on. They were drifting.

Show Illustration #10

They thought differently, surely, when they read in the letter: "Look to Jesus, the author and finisher of our faith . . .For the joy that was before Him, He endured the cross and despised the shame. Now He is seated at the right hand of the throne of God . . . Consider Him . . . He endured contradiction of sinners against Himself. Do not be weary and faint in your minds." (See Hebrews 12:2-3.) Forget yourself and your suffering. Think of the Lord Jesus and His suffering. And remember, it was the Lord God who laid on the Lord Jesus the sin of all of us. (See Isaiah 53:6; compare 1 Peter 2:24.) Your physical sufferings may be great. But His were greater. He, the holy, sinless One, took upon Himself the ugly, awful sin of all the world. Whenever you are treated badly and start feeling sorry for yourself, think of Him!

That was good advice for the suffering Hebrews. (And it is good for us, too.)

3. BELIEVERS MAY BE CAUGHT IN THE CURRENT BUT ARE FASTENED TO THE ROCK
Hebrews 13:5-9

A few of the Hebrew Christians had another problem. Some men had come teaching ideas which were not true. "Strange doctrines [teachings]" the letter-writer called them. (See Hebrews 3:9.) These men may have been the same false teachers who visited other cities. They had a set of laws which they insisted every Christian must follow. When the poor Jews tried to do so, they were completely confused.

Show Illustration #11

It was as if they had loosened their sail and were letting it flap–being blown this way and that. Each day they tried to follow some new law. They had trusted in the Lord Jesus alone for salvation. Now they thought that in order to keep their salvation, it was necessary to practice certain Jewish laws. So they were being tossed about.

God taught in the letter, "The Lord has said, 'I shall never leave you, nor forsake you.' So you may boldly say, 'I shall not fear what man will do to me . . . Jesus Christ [is] the same yesterday, and today, and forever.'" (See Hebrews 13:5-8.)

The ideas of men may change. The Lord Jesus never changes. By trying to add laws to God's gift of free salvation, Christians become confused. Remember this: the person who trusts in Christ is fastened to the Rock which cannot move. (In the illustration, do you see the rope holding the boat?) The Lord Christ is the One who said, "I give unto them eternal life; and they will never perish, neither will any man pluck them out of My hand" (John 10:29).

4. BELIEVERS ARE KEPT SAFE FOREVER BY THE CAPTAIN OF SALVATION
Hebrews 2:9-10; 7:24-25

Show Illustration #12

To get through rough waters, a ship needs a good captain. God has provided a Captain for the person whose trust is in the Saviour. That Captain is Christ Himself. (See Hebrews 2:10.) He knows every trouble each Christian will face. And He lives forever to pray for His own and bring them to His home safely. (See Hebrews 7:25.)

Until believers are with Him in His Heavenly home, they are to be busy here on earth. Take the Gospel to those who are outside of Christ ("outside the camp," 13:13), the letter says. Be willing to be laughed at by those who do not love Him. Continually thank God and praise Him (13:15). Do good to others. Share what you have (13:16). Obey those in authority over you (13:17). Pray for those who are serving the Lord (13:18).

These commands, written to the Hebrew Christians long ago, are also for us today. Are you taking the Gospel to others? Are you willing to be laughed at when you witness? Is your life full of thanks and praise to God? Are you doing good deeds for others and sharing what you have? Do you obey those who are over you? Are you praying for servants of the Lord?

If you must answer *no* to any of these questions, now is the time to change and get right with God. Please list in your notebook any matters which need attention in your life. Write down what you plan to do this week to follow these commands.

Lesson 4
THINGS THAT GO WITH SALVATION

NOTE TO THE TEACHER

Teaching others is a great responsibility. Immature teachers produce immature learners. Our students– and we teachers–should be growing spiritually. They may forget what we teach. They will remember how we live. The apostle spoke of this when he said, "Thou . . . who teachest another, teachest thou not thyself?" (Romans 2:21). He also wrote, "Be ye followers of me, even as I also am of Christ" (1 Corinthians 11:1).

This lesson is about growing up as Christians. We cannot feed others if we are not fed. We must spend time alone with God and His Word, asking Him speak to us and feed us.

Psalm 119 emphasizes the necessity of our feeding on God's Word which keeps us from sin (v. 11). It opens our eyes to eternal things (v. 18). It gives us understanding (v. 34). It is a light for our path (v. 105). It gives peace to those who love it (v. 165).

God says, "Let the word of Christ dwell in you richly . . . teaching . . . one another . . . singing with grace in your hearts to the Lord" (Colossians 3:16). As we study God's Word, we will become healthy, happy, growing Christians. May this be your experience.

Scripture to be studied: Hebrews 5:11—6:20

The *aim* of the lesson: To show the Christ responsibility in view of his eternal salvation.

What your students should *know*: Believers should grow in their Christian lives and bear fruit for God.

What your students should *feel*: Eager to feed on God's Word.

What your students should *do*: Set aside a portion of each day to spend time alone with God.

Lesson outline (for the teacher's and students' notebooks):
1. Salvation and growing up (Hebrews 5:11-14).
2. Salvation and building (Hebrews 6:1-6).
3. Salvation and fruit bearing (Hebrews 6:7-9).
4. Salvation and eternal safety (Hebrews 6:18).

The verse to be memorized:

How shall we escape, if we neglect so great salvation?
(Hebrews 2:3a)

THE LESSON
1. SALVATION AND GROWING UP
Hebrews 5:11-14

Do you have a baby in your home? How old he/she? What does he/she do? (*Teacher:* Encourage group discussion.) The Word of God tells us that Christians are like newborn babies.

Show Illustration #13

What food must a newborn baby have? (*Teacher:* Have students talk about a baby's need for milk.) God says, "As new babies, you should want the pure milk which is God's Word, so you will grow." (See 1 Peter 2:2.) A tiny baby is a delight. But if he/she is still tiny ten or 15 years later, he/she is pitiful.

Some of those who received the letter to the Hebrews had not grown spiritually (see 5:11-13). Many years had passed since they had received salvation. But they were not ready to learn more difficult truths about God. Such truths are spoken of as "strong meat" or "solid food." These people should have been grown-up teachers of the new Christians. They should have been eating solid food. (Do you see the man in the illustration?) Instead, they were like babies, waiting for someone to give them more milk. They wanted only the most simple Bible teaching–truths they already understood and were able to obey easily. What a pity! Year after year, they remained baby Christians. They never grew up.

"Solid food," God said in his message to the Hebrews, "is for the fully-grown" (See Hebrews 5:14.) A growing Christian who studies God's Word can tell the difference between right and wrong. As he learns new truths from God's Word and puts them to work, the child of God grows and grows in his Christian life.

2. SALVATION AND BUILDING
Hebrews 6:1-6

Have you ever seen men working on a new, big building? They begin with a good foundation.

Show Illustration #14

Lots of time is spent on the lower part of the building so the walls and roof will be firm and solid. Suppose the man in charge says, "Now that we have the foundation built, we shall tear it apart and start over. What has been done is all right. But we are going to begin again." What would you say if you were a workman? (*Teacher:* Let students discuss.) How would you feel if, after building it a second time, he would again insist that it be torn apart and made over? You probably would decide to work for someone else!

Well, some of the Hebrew Christians were having a similar problem. They were trying to lay again the foundation of their salvation. Imagine that! (See Hebrews 6:1-2.) They had turned to the Lord Jesus Christ. They had learned that He alone could save them. They had given up the ceremonies of the Jewish religion. They had been baptized to show others they belonged to the Lord Jesus. They understood that believers will live forever with the Lord. These truths were the foundation. Having known and accepted these teachings, they should have been building. As a building needs walls and a roof, so they needed to learn and practice additional truths from the Word of God. Instead, they were at the same place where they had begun.

3. SALVATION AND FRUIT BEARING
Hebrews 6:7-9

God wants each believer to be constantly growing in his Christian life. He wants baby Christians to become full-grown. He wants a building to have a good foundation with walls and a roof. He wants farms to yield good harvests.

Show Illustration #15

In the Hebrews' letter it was explained this way: Some ground soaks up the rain and splendid crops grow. Other fields get the same rain. But only weeds and thorns grow. Some who received this letter in the long ago are like many now. They were growing as Christians should. They shared with others who had needs (6:10). They helped those who were suffering for their faith in Christ. They were producing a harvest–a harvest of good deeds. God says such acts "go along with salvation" (v. 9).

Sad to say, some who read this letter had weeds and thorns instead of fruit in their lives. They lived much like the unbelievers around them. Their friends and relatives were coaxing them to return to their old religion. They were actually suffering because of their faith in God the Son.

The Lord reminded them that they simply had to trust Him. He listed many people, saying: "By faith Abel . . . by faith Enoch . . . by faith Noah . . . by faith . . .by faith . . . by faith." (See chapter 11.) "By faith these all did what I told them, trusting Me," God said.

Abraham was one He mentioned (11:8). When Abraham was old (age 75), God told him, "Get out of your country, leave your family . . . go to a land that I shall show you." (See Genesis 12:1-4.) Without even one question, Abraham obeyed God. He went, not knowing where the Lord would lead him. (See Hebrews 11:8-12.) God promised to give him and his son the land to which he was going. But Abraham did not have a son! Then the Lord God promised, "I shall give you a son." Abraham waited nearly 25 years before his son, Isaac, was born. All that time Abraham had only the promise of God. That was all Abraham really needed. And the Lord was pleased because Abraham believed Him. (See Genesis 15:6; Romans 4:3, 18.)

Do you trust God even when things seem dark and hopeless? When you are laughed at for talking to others about the Lord Jesus, do you still trust your Father in Heaven? Are you a fruitful, trusting Christian? Or is your life full of weeds and thorns and doubts?

4. SALVATION AND ETERNAL SAFETY
Hebrews 6:18

Hundreds of years before the letter to the Hebrews was written, the Lord gave His people some interesting instructions.

Show Illustration #16

God said to set aside certain cities. (See Numbers 35:1-34; Deuteronomy 19:1-21.) These were called cities of refuge (safety). If a person accidentally killed another, he ran as fast as he could to one of these cities. There he was safe. If he did not run, a relative (kinsman) of the slain person might kill him.

The Lord gave this example: Two men were cutting wood in the forest. The axe head flew off one man's axe and killed his friend. The killer was frightened and filled with remorse but he dared not stand around. He was in danger of losing his life by revenge. So he ran to the nearest city of refuge. There he was perfectly safe.

Those who have received God's gift of salvation are perfectly safe in the Lord Jesus Christ. He is the believer's place of refuge. (See Hebrews 6:18.) Jesus Himself said that those who trust in Him have "passed from death into life" (John 5:24).

How safe is the one who has fled to Jesus for refuge? He is as safe as the Lord Jesus. He saves "to the uttermost [fully and completely, for all time and forever] those who come to God by Him, because He lives forever to pray for them." (See Hebrews 7:25.)

How long will Jesus be with the believer? He said, "I will never leave you nor forsake you" (Hebrews 13:5).

Who provides eternal salvation? The Lord Jesus Christ. (See Hebrews 5:9.)

What price did He pay for our eternal salvation? His own precious blood. (See Hebrews 9:12.)

Have you received His salvation? If not, will you do so right now?

If you are a born-again child of God, are you growing in your Christian life? Do you spend time studying His Word? If not, will you promise Him right now that you will set apart a certain time each day to read the Bible and pray? (*Teacher:* Encourage students to write in their notebooks the time of day they will be in God's presence.)

Do you keep a notebook with your Bible? When God shows you in His Word something you should (or should not) do, write it in your notebook. Ask Him to help you do (or nor do) that thing.

For instance, in the book of Hebrews you see the warning against bitterness. (See 12:15.) Ask the Lord immediately to remove any wrong, bitter feeling you have against someone else. Then write in your notebook what you can do to conquer this sin. And seek to overcome it at once.

When you read, "Entertain strangers" (13:2), ask God to help you do this. Perhaps there will be a visitor in church whom you do not know. Does God want you to ask him to come to your house for a visit?

"Remember those in prison," you read (13:3). If you know someone in jail, write his name down. Decide what you can do for him.

"Remember those who are suffering because of something others have done to them." If you know someone who has been treated unkindly, promise God to help that person.

God will speak to you through His Word. His Holy Spirit living within you will help you to obey His Word. If you obey His Word, you will be a growing Christian. And if you are growing, God will teach you new truths from His Word–truths you can put into practice. The more you read, the more you will do, and the more you will grow. Then one day, when you are with Him forever, you will be a full-grown Christian. Think of that!

www.ingramcontent.com/pod-product-compliance
Lightning Source LLC
Chambersburg PA
CBHW060803090426
42736CB00002B/143